D0846260

THOMAS CRANE PUBLIC LIBRARY
QUINCY MA

CITY APPROPRIATION

SandCastle™

First Rhymes

The Chap
and the Cap

Mary Elizabeth Salzmann

Consulting Editor, Diane Craig, M.A./Reading Specialist

ABDO
Publishing Company

Published by ABDO Publishing Company, 4940 Viking Drive, Edina, Minnesota 55435.

Copyright © 2006 by Abdo Consulting Group, Inc. International copyrights reserved in all countries. No part of this book may be reproduced in any form without written permission from the publisher. SandCastle™ is a trademark and logo of ABDO Publishing Company.

Printed in the United States.

Credits
Edited by: Pam Price
Curriculum Coordinator: Nancy Tuminelly
Cover and Interior Design and Production: Mighty Media
Photo Credits: AbleStock, Eyewire Images, Liz Salzmann, Stockbyte

Library of Congress Cataloging-in-Publication Data

Salzmann, Mary Elizabeth, 1968-
    The chap and the cap / Mary Elizabeth Salzmann.
        p. cm. -- (First rhymes)
    Includes index.
    ISBN 1-59679-459-3 (hardcover)
    ISBN 1-59679-460-7 (paperback)
        1. English language--Rhyme--Juvenile literature. I. Title. II. Series.

PE1517.S3524 2005
808.1--dc22

2005047166

SandCastle™ books are created by a professional team of educators, reading specialists, and content developers around five essential components that include phonemic awareness, phonics, vocabulary, text comprehension, and fluency. All books are written, reviewed, and leveled for guided reading and early intervention reading, and designed for use in shared, guided, and independent reading and writing activities to support a balanced approach to literacy instruction.

Let Us Know

After reading the book, SandCastle would like you to tell us your stories about reading. What is your favorite page? Was there something hard that you needed help with? Share the ups and downs of learning to read. We want to hear from you! To get posted on the ABDO Publishing Company Web site, send us e-mail at:

sandcastle@abdopub.com

SandCastle Level: Beginning

-ap

cap

map

nap

snap

strap

Here is a  .

Look at the .

She takes a .

This is a .

See the  .

The cap is blue.

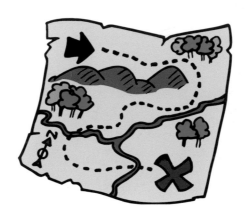

The map is old.

Tina takes a nap.

A snap has
two parts.

The strap is long.

The Chap
and the Cap

A young chap
found an old map.

The chap
made the map
into a cap.

18

The chap
put a long strap
on his map cap.

The strap that the chap
put on the map cap
has a silver snap.

The chap
wears his map cap
with the strap
and the snap
when he takes a nap!

About SandCastle™

A professional team of educators, reading specialists, and content developers created the SandCastle™ series to support young readers as they develop reading skills and strategies and increase their general knowledge. The SandCastle™ series has four levels that correspond to early literacy development in young children. The levels are provided to help teachers and parents select the appropriate books for young readers.

Emerging Readers
(no flags)

Beginning Readers
(1 flag)

Transitional Readers
(2 flags)

Fluent Readers
(3 flags)

These levels are meant only as a guide. All levels are subject to change.

To see a complete list of SandCastle™ books and other nonfiction titles from ABDO Publishing Company, visit **www.abdopub.com** or contact us at: 4940 Viking Drive, Edina, Minnesota 55435 • 1-800-800-1312 • fax: 1-952-831-1632